ESCAPE ARTIST

ESCAPE ARTIST

WITHDRAWN

TERRY BLACKHAWK

Winner of the John Ciardi Prize for Poetry
Selected by Molly Peacock

BkMk Press
University of Missouri-Kansas City

BkMk Press
University of Missouri-Kansas City
5101 Rockhill Road
Kansas City, Missouri 64110
(816) 235-2558 (voice)
(816) 235-2611 (fax)
www.umkc.edu/bkmk/
bkmk@umkc.edu

Cover image: Study for Painting with White Form, 1913
    Wassily Kandinsky, Gift of Mrs. Ferdinand Moeller
    Photo © 1985 The Detroit Institute of Arts
    Original painting: © 2003 Artists Rights Society (ARS),
    New York/ADAGP, Paris

Book Design: Susan L. Schurman
Managing Editor: Ben Furnish
Printing: Hignell Book Printing, Winnipeg, Manitoba

Thanks to Susan Cobin, Matt Ehrhorn, Greg Field, Lisieux Huelman, Jessica Hylan,
Jeannie M. Irons, Deborah Kroman, Elaine K. Lally, Philip Miller, Michael Nelson,
Linda Rodriguez, Maryfrances Wagner, Thomas Zvi Wilson

For information about the John Ciardi Prize for Poetry, contact BkMk Press. The prize
has been awarded previously to Steve Gehrke for *The Resurrection Machine*, selected by
Miller Williams, and to Tim Skeen for *Kentucky Swami*, selected by Michael Burns.

Library of Congress Cataloging-in-Publication Data

Blackhawk, Terry,
        Escape Artist/ Terry Blackhawk.--1st ed.
            p.cm.
Winner of the 2002 John Ciardi Prize for Poetry.
        ISBN 886157-40-5   (pbk. : alk. paper)
        I. Title.

PS3552.L34235E83 2003   2003007532
813'.54--dc21

10   9   8   7   6   5   4   3   2   1

This book is dedicated to my son,
Ned Blackhawk,
and to the memory of my mother,
Marie Woods Bohnhorst, 1923-2002.

Acknowledgements

Grateful acknowledgement is made to editors of the publications in which the following poems have appeared or are forthcoming:

Artful Dodge: "From the Östergötskan"; "Ex Machina: the Danish Museum"

CALYX: "What the Story Weaves, the Spinner Tells"

Controlled Burn: "Probe: Jody at the Open Mic" and "A Native of Damascus Regards the 'World Girls,' 1965"

Dispatch: DETROIT: "Orchis Opens the Book"

Ekphrasis: "Duende"; "Touchstone"; "Inventing the Torch"

English Journal: "Teaching with Dickinson One Morning in Spring"; "Shell Game"

Iris: A Journal About Women: "Daybreak Mix" and "..the days when Birds come back..."

Language Arts: "Repeating the Names of Signs"

The MacGuffin: "After Years of Ethnographic Research, Professor Jones Retires to the Tropics"; "Odysseus and His Men Pass the Sirens"; "Fire Dance"; "Capture"; "Moment of Breaking"

Maxis Review: "Parting the Waters"; "Against a Whiter Snow"

Marlboro Review: "Burmese Girls Sold into Prostitution in Thailand"

Michigan Quarterly Review: "For Dudley Randall"

Moving Out: "For Frona" (as "Bird Story")

Nimrod: "Mediterranean Crossing"

Poet Lore: "Amherst: Her Grave in Autumn"; "Between the Birds and Rauschenberg"; "Emily's Bee"

Rattle: "Compassion for the Minotaur"

Southern Poetry Review: "Escape Artist"

Sow's Ear Poetry Review: "Picking Olives on Kibbutz Geva"

Spoon River Review: "Good Friday at the Rookery"; "Marc Chagall's 'Green Violinist'"

U.S. 1 Worksheets: "St. Jerome in His Study"; "Amaryllis"

Visions International: "The Seal Wife"

The Year's Best Fantasy and Horror: "What the Story Weaves, the Spinner Tells"

"Good Friday at the Rookery" appears in *I Have My Own Song For It: Modern Poems of Ohio* (University of Akron Press)

"Burmese Girls Sold into Prostitution in Thailand" appears in *From the Breath of Parted Lips* (CavanKerry Press)

My heartfelt thanks, as always, to Judy Michaels, Elizabeth Socolow, Naomi Long Madgett, and Patricia Hooper. Thanks also to Ben Furnish, David Friesen and Susan Schurman for their tender care. I extend special gratitude to Molly Peacock.

CONTENTS

Let all things go free that have survived.
— Seamus Heaney

What the Story Weaves, the Spinner Tells

When I look out from inside
the dream and the space of the dream
shines between us, I see you there, shining

on the other side. The dream is a tale,
a story I tell, drawing us in to a new space,
encircling us in common light.

When everything vanishes but the light
of memory, what will protect us inside
our lines, this darkly echoing space?

Will it be the red handprint of our dreams
hovering over our heads, this thread of a tale
raveling, or the way I see your eyes shining?

Fisherman, you haul your nets in the shining
evening, your straining limbs pollinated by light.
Princess, you descend from the tower into the tale,

crumple, rise, redressed, victorious. Inside
our story, we do not live in grace but dream
of transformation, a new path to that open space

in the grasses where we reassemble our bones, pace
backward, then reclaim the panther whose shining
teeth dismembered the dimensions of our dream.

Third child, Grimm's little girl had it right: light
is the only way to fill us from the inside
out, the match in her apron pocket, the tale

a bright window against the black forest. We tell
and grow new with every telling, amazed by the space
we shape, the way we regard one another inside it.

1

Out of Bounds

Capture

Breath held at the drop/glide past my shoulder,
I imagine molten glass on a blower's rod,
and the sudden feathery fountain's a burst of fire
instead of this warbler splashing in the road.
Still as I stand, there's no real need for caution.
I could be a stump, a post to its fearless flight
above these ruts where I loom so huge and human.
But it's not the prothonotary's captured light
arrests me—
                  rather, a dark bulking thing
at the edge of sight so that almost without thinking,
I lift my glasses, fix, and find myself staring
into an owl's eyes; caught, as by the cruel remark
of a friend, stiff as the moth crumpled in its beak
as it swivels its head away, then gazes back.

Moment of Breaking

                              Nothing's where
it ought to be—these goblets you've found

shattered across her dressertop
the evening after your mother simply sat,
              leaned back, and died.

That the glasses broke—who can explain?
Two gray birds rise from your breast and disappear
              into the evergreens.

You see yourself, years ago, veering headlong down
the tallest dune—the submerged song of sand against sand,
              the wind a wet, rubbed

crystal rim as granules ground under your feet.
Then the laborious upward climb.   You puzzle at this
              sudden rearrangement:

the atomizer's useless bulb, misted drops
gone dry—all these glass collectibles you now imagine
              smashing. Sparks   rising gusts

of wind: you will release the fire-forged
ridges. The edges of the bright and singular shards splinter
              in your mind's eye and turn

infinitely small. To have this power. To hurl
and free each bound, annealed particle and be pierced at last
              at the moment of breaking

by a wild ringing, the dissolution of imprints
                        the pressed glass leaves.

At Boundary Bay

I've forded chest-high grasses
Onto posted land, torn webs
Of spiders bigger than my thumb,

Creatures who waved with small red claws
Like crabs crawled up from shore.
On this abandoned clamming ground,

I tower over kingdoms of periwinkles,
Crush seaworms' granular trails,
Each step erasing whole cities of snails,

But when my binoculars find him—
My goal, my grail, my short-eared owl—
I disregard destruction. Am I

Out of proportion? Out of bounds?
Behind him, Mount Baker's snowy sides
Gleam in waning light. Hovering,

Limned against this mother-of-pearl
Mountain of fire, his puffy flight
Makes a fine filmic moment

Until distances collapse, I'm slow
To stop motion and the frame
Eludes me. A bird may vanish into empty air,

But my footprints are everywhere:
A direct line back—clear evidence
Of the tangled brush I plowed through.

Shell Game

(for Tom)

What can fix a summer's focus
but the very ground creaking beneath us
releasing its parched hiss to the emerald leaves.

Make the light lime juicy, popsicle clean,
or say it was freighted with dust,
metallic on our tongues—it hadn't rained for days

that hot July I lined us up in order of height:
Philip Cohen, Ricky Reser, then Becky,
then you, my brother, smallest of *putti*,

your naked belly and drooping drawers
claiming the distinction of the rear.
Our mission—to circumnavigate the yard,

single file, leafmold scratching bare soles;
and what plodded out from dogwood shade,
stirred oakdust, painstakingly placed

one scaled foot in front of another—then played
dead until I grabbed it—but the treasure,
the creature, the prize.   Here, Tommy, I say,

you can carry the turtle. Small knight,
hapless button, your belly's a buzzing
morsel in the turtle's sight. Please point it

the other way, present a less tender target
to the beaked mouth, the thrust neck,
the prehistoric eye.   But tortoise strikes, grips.

Its hold becomes a story I almost manage
to forget until memory swoops down
from her branch, pecks at the armored shell.

And what animal would you choose to be,
little boy? *Wipe scars clean, they disappear.*
Let bait and switch teach you about trust,

how years after the pliers, the hurled
shattering of shell from a father's furious arm,
a crablike pinch remains.

Beware of sisters bearing gifts. Don't go
shirtless in the heat. Turn a tortoise
upside down. Listen for the rain.

Escape Artist

A crow does not merely open its beak to cry
or sing, but presses its whole body forward,
playing itself like a bagpipe, pumping out
cranky, cranked-up rhythms. Early March,

branches bare of all but these new tenants
whose raucous calls begin well before dawn,
who daylong wheel from here to Bretton Drive,
conducting their business on our lawns.

All week I've watched them, filling our neighbors' trees,
displacing the air with their caws, less flock
than visitation. To my friend who'd have it
that the crow is negation made manifest—

a thing with claws that perches on her shoulder,
reciting endless tapes of whoever teased, carped,
hurt, abused—I'd say send those sad tales
through the maw of a ventriloquist's doll, a human

puppet she alone controls. For who can manage
the wild lift of wings? Who pass through the dark
windows crows place against the sky? If there's limit
in what we say, each word a fence or boundary,

it must be why the crows have gathered and gone now.
I miss the rough rush of their risings up and settlings down,
and that one I saw on Lancashire, dangling by its left foot
upside down from a wire. Electrocuted, I thought,

surely dead, the dank, bone-filled rag of it—
until it swiveled upright, flapped, then flew, glad,
I suppose, to have looked at the world in a new way,
to be leaving behind a dummy's point of view.

Mirror Surface

How difficult to paint one's own portrait Van Gogh said,
but here's my blind contour mind tracing the pen as the pen
casts its shadow across the page, luscious shadows—
I cannot name them enough, the coverlet that catches them
in pools along the stitching, soft undulant folds the afternoon sun
plays over warmly, waxily, as if drawn by a creamy crayon.
I love their blur, smudge, overlap, the edge effect that helps me
enter sideways this one singular moment. Then the shine,
the patina he achieved by using a wash of milk, and the wash itself,
the rush of words across the page, spilling, reshaping
as soon as they're down, leading me skipping... ahead? into what?
Some door I'd open? A newly surfaced road? Yesterday,
through the rainy afternoon, the road was a mirror, and I was planing
maybe an inch above it, enjoying the fine floating feeling
while on the car radio the surfer shouted "Surf's up!" and I wanted
to be gliding with her. Hard enough to catch the wave of this pen,
fingers fly, or try to, skimming ahead of all the trips
I'll never take, ignoring the obvious robin outside my window
as I recall a rain-laden branch, its thwack/slap on my windshield
and I slowed, downshifted, wondering what new world rolled
ahead of and beneath my tires, Rosedale Park so green and full
of trees, Bretton Drive's fresh asphalt smoothed with rain.
I looked up by looking down, trees mirrored in the black
surface, the upside down cumulus of them, their inverted silver-greens
and blue-greens becoming a submerged reef, a sunken cathedral,
drenched, shining. It was Monet now, above and below, it was echoing
chords, the beautiful blur and blurring of heavily weighted clouds
of maples and elms, and I was happy, saturated, suspended in between—
trying to go as slow as I could, wanting not to arrive anywhere,
to remain lost in the raveling scrawl, the brainy shapes of the trees.

Repeating the Names of Signs

At eight I sang the signs I saw:
painted rocks and Burma Shave.
The landscape flipped by in a blur
of twisting mountain roads
in southern Tennessee, *Chenille*
For Sale, Jesus Saves, and mules
breathing into opening pastures.

Singing, singing, my head
pressed to the window of the aging
Chevy, I wished to go unnoticed
and read my world like a rebus:
whatever some farmer plastered
or sprayed on barn or fence
was stuff enough for me.

But let no adult find me cute.
My song was not for anyone else,
that record flashing by,
words formed aimless as balloons,
the story waiting to complete itself
around the nearest turn.

For Frona

Your mother's eyes are ringed now
and like the rings within a tree
betray her age, her retina
decayed beyond repair.

She tells me she can see
only the periphery of things
and she inclines her head
to bring my face in focus.

She's always loved the birds
but now you must explain
even the commonest ones that come
to share the seed you scatter.

I've often wondered where you
came by your sense of story,
and when she tells how,
on a northern lake, paddles raised,

the only sound the drip
of water from the blades—
how there, in that hush,
the guide pointed out

the flaming red head
and bright black back
of the great pileated woodpecker—
I think I know.

I've never seen that bird,
yet there it sits, in its shyness,
us whispering, drifting by
these fifty years.

11
DEPARTURE AND RETURN

Picking Olives on Kibbutz Geva, 1965

Two mouths pressed one pomegranate.
Two heads ascended into the green
branches, peered through the dusty leaves.
But just one voice remains and what were
the words I saw through then
those aleph and beta afternoons we sat
on the *ulpan's* wooden benches, *shiksas*
learning the lessons of a new land and language.

Not branch, dust, sun, shadow
nor the feta cheese we ate before dawn.
Nor the lizards freeze-framed at my reach
those orchard mornings, sun rising
behind us, our hands pulling down
and along the wand-like twigs.
How easily olives detach from their stems,
plop like soft rain into canvas buckets.

Across the Valley of Gilead, the Spring of David
had flowed for countless thousand years,
but already the friend I journeyed with
has disappeared. Now my fingers sift
those autumn months, stir pebble-like fruit,
some green, some stained purple, remembering
how I could pierce one with a thumbnail,
release a creamy oil to soothe aching hands.

At harvest this fruit is never palatable.
It's my job to collect, never to taste.
I readjust the burden basket, try to recall
exactly how the canvas straps
fit across my shoulders, but the pattern's
as closed as the doors of the *kibbutzim*
protecting their privacy, or the story
of that old man in the leather shop.

Viewing the numbers tattooed on his arm
I felt like an intruder, witness to what
I shouldn't see. They'd haul bushels of fruit
away on tractors to be steamed,
steeped in spices and brine.
I'll never forget his arm, how the ink,
like the purple mottling an olive,
seemed to have blurred beneath the skin.

Between the Birds and Rauschenberg

Rauschenberg's stencilled signs say STOP!
ONE WAY. DO NOT STAND ON END. So I stop
For his neon eagle with its claws clasped
Around a crystal ball, just as I stopped
On oil-soaked streets for children with filmy eyes,
Sliding slim fingers into *gringa* pockets.

I bid farewell to easy *sucres*, sugar money
Loose and fluty as Andean notes drifting
Toward cloud forests whose far-off
Greens now complement these reds
And golds, reds on gold, blood-red gauze
And gilded wings under his epoxied glaze.

I went to Ecuador to lose my way
In the language of birds and native magic.
Scarcely home again, touring this exhibit,
What's present and what's after-image
Seem to overlap. Tropic mnemonics pop up
Their heads, scuttle out from collages

Busy as the head-bobbing tinamou,
The raucous chachalaca. Between
Silk-screened campesinos and the shellacked
Cardinal spray-painted black, I stoop
To peer into A CAGE TO CATCH THE WITCH.
Duck! I think, though she's not here.

Was it she I saw in Coca shuffling
Toward that terrace where captive birds
Sent water dishes clattering to the floor?
The empty cage provides NO PUBLIC SHELTER.
Did she EXIT via this ladder
Rauschenberg mounted on the wall?

Her job, to restore the birds to order.
To return them to their perches
In the hotel garden. To chase down the freedom-
Seeking parrot slinking across the tiles,
Clipped wings tight against its sides.
I wanted to tell the parrot: Hurry. Hide!

You will find no public shelter.
Skirt the woman. Avoid gun-toting
Youths who parade the veranda
In high-laced boots. In the true wild,
One is seldom attacked by wild things.
This is what the healer explained, waving

A lemon-scented branch while dancing
Columns of bees, drunk on their own honey,
Ignored him. So I try to ignore army
Helicopters hovering in silent drone
Above the canvas surface. LAY OUT STRETCHER
ON FLOOR. MATCH MARKINGS AND JOIN.

Forget the soldiers who searched my bags,
Pawed my belongings. Recall how orchids
Can thrive at high altitudes even on the Mountain
Of Fire, how there are many routes
Through the jungle. Sometimes a sudden explosion.
Puff of smoke above the canopy of trees.

Burmese Girls Sold into Prostitution in Thailand

"We make our story something to envy, so we are not left with nothing."

In order that her parents not go deeper into debt
       she does not kill herself, she is
the bargain, the chip, she evens
       the odds even though she cannot speak
the language, Thai, it misaligns her tongue, sounds
       oily to her ears, the tongues of men, the forcing
of them, hundreds, thousands, how many
       places can they find on her, the body has only
so many openings and she loses
       value quickly once twice maybe three
times she can be passed off
       as a virgin even as she faints, even as she
counts the bricks in the windowless
       walls, corridors where she never sees
the sun unless—to settle the madam's score—she is
       arrested, hauled out from the underground
cells—then only the quiet ones are not
       redeemed, the ones who do not
know how to smile at men, but she is
       ransomed back to the metal
bed, the cement floor, the men again and
       again, especially the drunks
frighten her, so she feels nothing, nothing
       when the child moves inside her, nothing
when the poison she takes flattens
       her belly so that another girl will never
be born to turn eleven or twelve into nothing
       of value but the stories she makes even when
the fatigue claims her and she is coated with sores and
       sent back to her village where she is
whispered about, no friends, nothing
       but these mascara'ed eyes, this fringed
cloth embroidered with tales of luxury rides
       bringing the city to the village in a voice
hardened to the waste the man in her dreams
       who appears dressed in red brings—
until fevers overtake her and her
       mouth turns dry and she is
so thin the wind blows through her until she is

parched, barely bones and so little flesh
left for the pyre, but they burn her body anyway, let
flames rise around her, the heel the strongest
glowing coal, a searing eye watching back at
them a long time as they burn all that is
hers: the city clothes, the plastic shoes, the drinking cup.

Trompe l'Oeil Variations

(Alan Huber Lloyd, composer and artist, 1942-1986)

i. Brick Effect

When you couldn't chip through the painted
plaster to reach the mortared bricks beneath,
you picked up palette and brush, oils
and enamels to create your own brick effect.

It lit a spark among your friends until
every surface and frame in that sixth floor walk-up
burgeoned with ferns, tendrils, butterflies, bees.
No special come-on the way the bower bird

feathers his bower, just this ornate time
capsule, florid snow globe, missing story
with its too few bits to shake, savor, the shell
long since cracked, the building razed.

ii. The Unleaving

Bleak March in New York yet you saw nothing
but gold: autumn's blaze across the East Side's
rooftops. "The leaves are so lovely this fall,"
Kenneth, keeping watch, heard you say.

Reverse the cleaver, I think. Drop this
armload of books to the floor, one for each year
you've been gone and I've gone on assuming
you, still there, somewhere. Spared.

It was not some trompe l'oeil leaf you saw gleaming
against the bricks. It was nothing enough to hold you
into life or me into belief in its lastingness.
The fall would come, regardless of the season.

iii. Altered States

When you died your friends rushed to light
incense, raise windows, clear the air
of hash and weed, hushed and awed surely
yet conspiratorial in grief, circling you
with votive candles—the warmth still on you,
a new-found light seeping into my dreams
so that lately I return to the campus of our youth,
its tower and glen. Last night, it was
wedding-cake modern, everything had changed,
and I was no longer enrolled in that dream.

I guess it's because you've woven into
my mind at last—rumpled hedonist,
a slightly dazed, pot-blissed Christ awash
in bedsheets in the photo Ken sent
on the Internet, your image filling the screen
so suddenly it's hard not to wonder
if you're not still out there or why
you return to me now, thirty years later,
thirteen of them dead. In Perugia
you painted your dream again and again,
each day variations on the same pomegranate.

Now, whatever recurs, nothing's exact,
not the finch flying free from its cage
in your room, not the bicycle built for two
your parents were pleased to launch us on
as we careered, secretive and stoned
around those well-laid lawns, the antique
silver inside neither of us would inherit.
Yesterday, in the MRI, its jack-hammer pulsing
inches from my ear, I was glad for the altered
states we'd visited, those Spanish-Tibetan borders

outside your windows on East Fifth Street,
and the close-up looks you taught me
as we peered into tide pools or stared late at night
studying the flashing of the IRT. What happened
to your theories—how drone turns to pattern,
incites a cellular music, buzzing focal points
I recalled as the magnet pounded
in my head and I saw dancers, bodies caught
by space and sound, costumed not in cloth

but shimmer, sine curves, waves of monomaniacal

beats so loud it was not my own cells'
treachery obsessed me, but this news of you —
an elastic stretching forward and back,
a forgotten box, a woodpecker drumming,
a hinge repeating *gone, gone, not gone,*
gone. The trees have not forgotten you
came to me through the drone,
and I wanted so much to believe in the trees,
when the pounding stopped I longed for the waves
to pull me in again.

iv. Rock and Carry

Not the way lovers breathe, exactly, but like the companions
we were, compadres who joked in a foreign tongue and tossed

theories whimsical as air—it was that breath again, Alan,
last night, after the conference, when I sat, transported,

in a circle with strangers, letting words rock and carry me,
like the train in the poem of that young man, whose voice and eyes

surely were yours, no matter the passage of years. In his lines
I heard decades click by—rails, countries, stanzas filled

with medieval bell towers and landscapes tilled
according to ancient patterns. Now I wonder what will provide

enough pulse or breadth to pull me upward and out
like your paisley bedspread that doubled as a curtain, how it swelled

from your dorm window as if propelled by the sonatas
you played behind it. I would gladly fall from that window,

spill backward reeling in the trust that memory, or even
my forgettings, will catch me—the way his poem's rhythms led me

along our path through the Glen to the ledge overlooking the marsh
where redwings nested and you sketched and interrogated them,

giving them back their whistles, their song, just as I would give back
whatever it meant to be your friend then, or to sit last night

in a badly lit room at a table round as a rim, a nest,
listening intently to our words, our pages fluttering

back to that sketchbook you carried whose every leaf and rock,
cliff and tide pool created its own force-field, a place where clam

became cloud became thumb-shadow, shoulder of wing, echoes
I could almost see on the page, shimmery contours, traces of hand tracing

object, vision, the sound of a train, the friend growing smaller
in the station, steam in the spaces between the observed, the felt thing.

v. Good Friday at the Rookery

Through the intervening scrim
        of last year's leaves and vines
their nests seem like mistletoe,
        or clouds, and the traffic's din
mutes their flight to pantomime.

If only I could hear them. If only I could
        assert some selective silence.
I want the geese to stop their territorial
        announcements and the peepers
cease their high-pitched calls

so that I may listen in on the dance
        of the herons' mating. I want to cross
the fence and step deeper into the swamp
        until the traffic on this two-lane road
fades away. May the dying out of engines

be the last dying. No more vans of visitors
        or Harleys revving slowly
through the dry spring air. Just these birds'
        balancing acts on platforms
in the unleafed sycamores. I want to hear

the flutter of the male as he lands feet first
        as if stretched by some string along
the vertical. I want the click of twig on beak
        as she accepts his one single stick
after each lift-off and return.

No more cries from noisier creatures.
        No more bleats from the beasts
of Kosovo tethered in their burning stalls.
        I want to understand only this:
how he plummets to the swamp floor,

then hoists his crook-necked glide into
        ever-widening rings, how when he
mounts her, his wings exalt the air.
        Only this, until the egg is ready
to burst its shell. Then I will sketch

these birds the way Alan did who died
over a dozen Easters gone.
I will use his unerring lines to show
how the female's crown
feathers above the thorns of the nest.

With luck, I will conjure
some mad trompe l'oeil
to fool *eye and* ear and let me hear
his vanished music.
Then I will invite them all back in—

the loudmouthed geese, ululating frogs,
folks treading gravel alongside
the road—I will bring them all in to inhabit
my wavery lines and his ink-
dark pools, the space of his unframed page.

"...the days when Birds come back..."

—Emily Dickinson, J 130

When she heard the first
cardinal sing, right on time
as January lapsed and February
began, she did not think of the wheelchair,
useless on its peg in the garage next door,
or the friend's forehead she had kissed
for the last time, or the stories
they'd shared not because
they loved gossip so much but rather
for the exchange itself, the rise
and fall of their voices, the pulling
of figures from everyday lives
as scarves from a sleeve, the pure
transformative pleasure of "No!
he didn't!" or "Yes, she did"—
chords of delight or envy
that plunked across the drive
between them like notes from the piano
the friend had moved years ago
into the living room, keys
the husband would come to press
night after night in the empty room,
tunes more deliberate and less
harmonious than the musical
laugh that no longer rises
from sidewalk or backyard
or the red bird's pouring song.
She recalled instead how a year
had passed since her friend first
knew it was time—declaring
"This is getting old"—and how,
at the very end, the waiting
face composed itself into
its final mask in a manner
as punctual and surprising
as the departure and return
of the birds.

Teaching with Dickinson One Morning in Spring

i.
Steer from your blind side,
I tell them; try not looking
too directly at any single thing.

But Josh's t-shirt turns my eye: *Focus
on the River*. Although the calendar says
May, the morning starts slowly—

with questions leading up her sparsely lit stair.
They're nervous at first, reticence
like staves to arrange their notes upon—

& they follow her rhythms, even against their will.

ii.
Breeze from the window, fresh tune
on the stair. Stair as words to scratch,
rearrange. Stair as their new lines rising

from her not-so-old text:
less a spiral than a wild
geometry, with platforms, landings

Escher-tricky: follow the lines,
mount the steps, arrive at the crossroads
of Paradox & Immortality—

but that flood's a subject that's rising, rising...

iii.
and me, I'm focusing on
the river, *the old—road—through pain—*
Like these students, I have many questions:

How is a mustard a metaphor?
Where does time come from? And Larry,
what could I have told him,

who last year sat not far from this classroom
in a garden by the river, watching the rushing
water, lilies of the valley sweetening

the last spring he'd ever know?

Amherst: Her Grave in Autumn

Despite a sun almost down, I aim
my camera carefully.
At its interloping buzz, juncos scatter

to the evergreens. Nearby, maples
flame, but within her wrought-iron fence
the cedar does not change.

Compassed, drawn by this last
whetstone for her will,
it's my privilege to scrutinize.

Eye and ear mix
bird and tree: chips scissor the branches,
suggest the flowers, gestures

of a skillful hand.
The bloom lurks
within the bulb, the bulb within

the earth, the song
within the bird.
Called back to this spare plot,

granite name,
I count October tributes—
coins, strips, statice

tied with thread. The tombstone top's
a lip of bloom
here, where speculation ends.

III

WHAT THE STORY WEAVES

Luck

As the throb of the fan lulls us to sleep
and the sky clears of its ragged green
curtain of clouds, we breathe a simple

peace free of the storm that twisted and snapped
a waist-thick branch from our silver maple
          and flung it across the yard
against the wind's direction.

We measured our luck then, plunging
arms shoulder-deep into a hole in the ground
we could have found in the roof above
          our bedroom ceiling.

Knock wood, pinch salt: tonight
our luck's nothing more tangled
than our limbs, sated and safe
beneath the unbreached plaster.

Tomorrow I'll step into the rainwashed air,
chin high with relief, not hunkered
like some medieval Eve cringing into
the unexpected world, not like that couple

we found last summer having sex
in the abandoned lighthouse.
I can still see them hopping into
their clothes, covering their crotches

as if a sword-bearing angel pursued them.
Their footprints in the muddy path
from the parking lot out to the beach

made a story we'd later reconfigure
after coming on the luck of its surprise ending:
his bare bum and her quivering thighs.

Turning quick to save them from embarrassment,
I thought Erie's windblown waves
drowned out my retreat. Luck's
my chance now to say I was not

a tormenting angel, not a storm-bearing cloud.
I was shushing Evan, backing away
into the woods, trying to protect them,

when they flushed into the open
like a couple of quail, fleeing the earth
they'd pressed for us to see.

Daedalus Remembers

If only memory would stumble, unwind
on itself, become a labyrinth of reversals—
I would gladly enter. Let words and thoughts
switch places, topple like stones
which is how I recall him,

clumsily trying to read
the simplest plan. When he'd sound
those words he'd almost gasp for air.
Ba-bar-barm-le-bar... MAR-BLE.
I could chisel lines faster than he

could say them, my poor, slow child,
though I guess I deserved him: the axe
that never hewed straight in his hand, all his
patterns smudged—penance perhaps
for my murderous pride.

Muted by confinement, his hours luxurious
but dim, the sun reached him from only the highest
windows. And always the monster's roars—
yet at times Icarus approached the beast
to mutter and rock their common woe.

He asked for little so where he got it
amazed me—the dream, the idea of flight.
Maybe from some gull winging past, translucent
as a vision he couldn't express.
But he set me to it — oh heart,

artifice — to design our way out!
A secret he kept easily, he with few words
to begin with, so when we mounted
the cliff that shone like marble
and stood there in the altar of the air,

imagine my surprise as words
began streaming from him: *iceberg, aurora,*
clamor, drop-off... He teetered
and I swore it was a babble of altitude
or else the pouring light, impossible

sun drenching us, but cold and still
he would not stop spinning his chatter of chill
        and excitement. All I could do was watch
                him tug the straps against the whining wind
                        as he hopped and pulled and the wings banged

                like shutters and yes, yes, he seemed to listen,
but it was cold and bright and he could barely wait.
        Father, thunderstorm, needlenose, nightmare
                he laughed, launching himself toward the warmth,
                        my bird, my futile caution.

Compassion for the Minotaur

We need it
for the same reason
we say we grieve—for ourselves,
not for those who've gone.
For nights when touch isn't enough
and a partner's peaceful breath
will not lure us into sleep
but we must stare out at the room
unable to name the dark
while all we've tried to hide
roars up from the basement
and follows us when we step outside
ourselves, so that we hear,
in the traffic's whine
or the homeless man's rage
that echoes through the tunnels of the MTA,
the same despairing bleat
that must have burst from the snout
of the helpless baby
when he saw his mother's
horrified gaze and understood
that it fell on no gleaming hide
or ears sweet to scratch
but a creature angular and strange
whom she could not possibly cradle,
or croon to, or take as her own.

The Seal Wife

His vision blurs as if cauled or dimmed
by too much seeing. Where he lives
no trees interrupt the horizon
and his view dissolves to grief
like a seabird's drifting call. Waves
pound his beach, cold, hard as a skull.

He recalls how he dropped tackle and scull
that night by the rock as sunset dimmed
when he saw her naked, staring at the waves
as her brothers dived into their lives
without her, abandoning her to grief
for her lost pelt and known horizon.

To him she meant warmth, a horizon
of possibility, his pounding skull
song rescued at last from the grief
of his empty hands: his damned, dimmed
luck. He would take her and their lives
together would flout the cruel waves.

But who would she be with no waves
to enfold her? The horizon
numbs her, seems to flatten their lives.
Her brothers' names she can barely recall.
Without her fur, she feels dimmed,
peeled, not quite human in her grief.

As their children arrived, her grief
ebbed somewhat, like waves
at sunrise, phosphorescence dimmed,
until one August moon cleared the horizon
and kindled a flame in her skull:
she'd unbraid her twisted lives.

Seal sister, human mother, she lives
between land and sea. He'd locked her grief
in his wooden box: her skin, her sculp—
she'd find it, then leave him, without a wave
goodbye, to scan a mute horizon,
crying out for her until his voice dimmed:

"Who lives with you beneath these waves
knows neither love nor grief..."   The horizon
echoed "Rascal" as his heart's fires dimmed.

"Daybreak Mix"

In her dream she confused armadillo
and watermelon, watched the fruit waddle
across the road while the creature rolled
into a pond and bobbed there like a huge,

unhatched egg. Now she walks the morning
market, trying to sort produce from purchase,
and this new plant whose name has her
almost on her knees, peering nose-close

into flats of daisy-eyed plants as if she could
parse their petals, get a fix on the air
between syllables that dance a drunken
Break! *Mix*! and *Day-ay-ay-O*!

"It's a ground cover," the grower assures her.
And, "yes, if you plant it, it'll do well,
like anything." Okay, so maybe she'll take it, home,
like anything. She knows luck's not much more

than a stone removed from her shoe, a bad dream
dismissed before it's understood, and lately
she's ducked through pauses in her speech as if
the wrong noun were about to switch lanes

and bear down on her. She'd avoid,
if she could, the attachment of words to things—
but even as she quarrels with the dark, the sky
slips into place, noon arrives in a burst,

and the market becomes so present and palpable
she thinks she might recover the known,
can set no higher sights than these clusters
of beets and onions gleaming in the sun.

Today she'll seek no castles vanishing
into the thin air of middle age. Enough,
this farmer calling "Star fennel, cilantro,
fern leaf dill" and explaining how heliotrope

is Greek for "sun's flower." Not sunflower,
but *sun's* flower, from a time when sun meant

God and flower must have meant meaning—
trope-ical, tropical.... Oh, there's no heat rising,

just the vanilla scent of the heliotrope
whose purple petals form a kind of fringe.
"Lace," she might have called it once.
"Once upon a time," she might have said.

Orchis Opens the Book

of animal castration.
She knows it's not about pain,
rather convenience and ancient
practice: diagrams of restraint
and genitalia opposite
instruments of sterility
curving like saracen moons.
Crescent, nascent—she doesn't
look too closely. There's no blood
to speak of and what's implied
has little to do with husbandry.
The denuded bellies and poor,
clipped bulbs remind her
not of absence, but tulips—
the ones she rushed last fall
into almost frozen ground.
Flags of hope, it's been a long winter.
She wants to watch each stalk
thrust open, unfurling first
as fringes then flaring, loudmouthed
cups of bloom. Petals like hide,
she will see them rise,
feel the earth whinny and stomp.

After Years of Ethnographic Research, Professor Jones Retires to the Tropics

Don't get me wrong.
Just because you see me
tying on this sarong
doesn't mean the seamy
sides of these natives'
lives entice me,
or their soft culture—
all fronds and coconuts, knives
slicing down the moisture-
laden fruit that drips
sweetly from my lips.

So, yes, I guess
I've become a kind of fixture
here, my loosened dress
disguising nonetheless
an academic heart. But where's
that gone? Here, where air's
hibiscus mild, I seem to lose
my rubrics, notes, and plans.
I take in a new world's news
on palmy sands.

But isn't this after all
what I've tried to teach my
students hunkered, fall
and winter long? Open your eyes!
I tell them. Put on an alien
point of view. Make foreign skin
the way you let your data come in.

Like the waves around my toes—
these, too, a proper tool
for research—the endless flow's
a pattern you won't learn in school.
I tell them that as well.
Transcribe everything? Yes, I say.
You want your subjects natural,
have done your best to allay
their charming, native naivete?

Then, of course, record. But tie
the knot however you can.
Do *and* record. No need to buy
smiles from that bronzed young man.
Like yours, his heart's as free
as his warm pacific glance.
Go to it now. You're trained to see—
you're honed with sensitivity.
Pursue each fine nuance.

Odysseus and His Men Pass the Sirens

The idea was to test himself, in bondage,
like Prometheus, though he'd never be so lamblike—
no self-sacrificial gouging for him. He'd clench
his jaws, grit fiercely. He'd have control.
And there it was. Control. The beauty of it.
For once they saw they'd never have him,
how they'd pour out their passion, lavishing him
with honeyed tones, oh droning bees, oh sweetest
gardens laden with longing. How strict he'd hold
against them, bound beyond himself. How easy
to outwit them with his helplessness.

                    Consider, then, Odysseus,
lashed upon the mast. The deck pitches. The men
pull harder. "Stroke!" he exhorts them.
"Eyes forward!" Of course the men can't hear him.
But what do they feel beyond the beating waves?
Do they pause and lift their oars
and let the trireme founder to take a free,
collective glance across the whirling sea?

By now the hero sees nothing. His eyes roll
heavenward. He writhes and rails but the thongs
hold. It all holds. There is nowhere to go
but onward. Yet in that moment before they
shoulder the blades and find the forward rhythm,
don't the men catch one another's eyes?
Don't they exchange at least one knowing, sweating grin
as they turn and glance back at him, flush
against the mast, senseless in glory, his erect sex
breaching his garb as he aches to burst into that song?

Probe: Jody at the Open Mic

Beyond the mic—a surge of shapes and shoulders,
cubes and planes like my body on canvases
of the would-be artists I work for.
To them I'm nothing more than an apple on a plate,
but here's a different stage.

Quick change, I shake off flicks
against my skin and try to forget
what I can't ignore: the squat man who burst forth
and put his fingers in all my wrong
places. Semiautomatic,

semi-autic, my words probe the room
the way my little car moved that day
through a convoy of tractor-trailers,
a rolling canyon of semis, mud-flaps
with silhouetted dollies, boobs erect.

I'm hiding out in this spotlight, exposed
as well as disguised. What can these folks know
of how I wrinkle old men between my fingers
then deposit them like broccoli
at the bottom of a tray?

I'm the girl in the long dress with the china eyes.
I make the current exchange.
My clothing wears like a second
layer of skin. And if I trusted the wrong person,
someone who gave me only what I wanted

to hear—cowboy twang, that meanness on the wind—
it thrilled me and I longed to drive, plunge
directly over the edge,
be seduced, wherever his traffic
would take me. Kansas or Paris, maybe.

I hardly know what I feel now,
pitching words like some sucker
at a midway ring toss,
hoping for luck from these weak sisters,
understudies for the real action.

The mic's got its oily smell and behind me
the sound system creates a gap between
what I say and what I hear, an echoing
lag between speech and sound—
space enough to get lost in.

IV

AN EARLIER TONGUE

Mediterranean Crossing, 1965

Tossed out of sleep by a midnight gale,
I've hurried up through passageways
from my tiny cabin five decks below.

Leafed among the pages of Kafka's
Letters to Milena I was reading at the time
I can still find the cartoon
that the Dutch journalist I'm about to meet

sketches on a cocktail napkin
during the conversation we're about to have:
Hitler's caricature, his own design.

He's proud of this underground Kilroy
that twenty years before appeared on walls,
leaflets, the goofy moustache
and rabid eyes emblems of Resistance news.

We're the only passengers in the salon,
munching crackers, trying to stay the storm
in our stomachs.   Thirty-foot seas are
routine to the waiter in his rumpled jacket

so I know we will not need to
flee to the indifferent lifesavering shippen.
"Keep eye on horizon," the waiter says, "you okay.
You keep balance. No sick. No sick."

I can't recall the Dutchman's face
but back in that weather-wracked time capsule
I find him still flirting with the dangers

he so eagerly imparts—betrayals, escapes,
grenades disguised as potatoes in children's baskets;
and he's flirting with me, in my beatnik turtleneck,
and I'm drinking it in.   Solitary traveler,

I'm feeling smooth and savvy and grown
until a confessional gleam freezes in his eye.
"We had to do"—here his voice drops—"many things,"
and he tells me about the double agent he seduced,

then had assassinated. I look away,
searching for the line between water and sky.
"She was so young," he says, "and beautiful."

St. Jerome in His Study

(after Van Eyck)

Is a smile tracing his lips, or simply
an inkling of perfection, the immaculate
arrangement of his cape, his brass-bound box,
his mind? Within this mahogany chamber
does he dream of desert nights
or noontime suns when even the serpent
sought shelter in the shade?

Of all places on the planet, he would choose
the most empty, an enviable limitlessness,
yet there, too, a cell of sorts contained him.
Five years in the desert. An iconography
for any artist to draw upon: a treasury
of hourglass, pomegranate, of swift conversions
from Hebrew to Latin, daylight to evening,

thought to mind. It's hard to imagine him
this composed and reflective as he searched
each day's translation, paced, gestured, swapping
verbs, genitives, haggling for fair exchange
as surely as olive merchants shuttled
their amphorae across the waters, trailing
in their unwitting wakes the latest in art,

weaponry, or fashion. No rose windows then,
just the hardscrabble cave, dust and the text,
its supply of demands: syllables to wrestle,
nuggets to test against his reserve:
that place of peace where he was always
a shade removed from himself, mindless
of the dervish winds, the dividends of stars.

From the Östergötskan

Tonight the moon's a clock
poised above the cathedral's grill-worked
spire. Late, but it's light—a drawn-out
mid-June night and all the archipelago
ablaze in our eyes as we push
out from the tavern
into the cobbled streets. Is it thin air
keeps us barely ballasted, these ballads
we hum, or faith, that Gothic
hour hand pointing to the sky?

Some nights we think anything
could happen, here at the top of the planet,
the tilt end of the century.
And why not wish
for the needle to widen its eye,
or the moon
to thread that steeple
whose intricate ironwork
sieves the midsummer air?
How subtly it sifts
the insubstantial light
like lace on the window
beside our aging mother
stitching at hearthside, loaves
on the table, sentiment,
all the rest. She'd tell us
to paint our houses
red against the cold, make from scratch
what we can, name the plants
in our garden in Latin as well
as our earlier tongue.

Nearby, the abbey, ruined, bare
where Birgit prayed
until her knees
wore indentations in the stone.
Now her bones, those
fragmented sisters,
are on display across the continent.
Like her, we could turn into
talismans. Or swans.

But if we feel ourselves rising,
floating within, we only toast
expansion. What else to do
but button again against our raw
skinned selves, our shyness
thick as slabs of bread, a common
flavor, slowly chewed.

Ex Machina: The Danish Museum

No clock's stopped. No hand's rewound the hour's
arrows. Just the washer's clanking, off-center
spin which stalls on the verge between rinse and dry
with such thudding suddenness it must be why
I see myself staring again at that small Rococo dome,
its surface so bespeckled and beswirled
it couldn't have been a model of the world.

No photo exists and the friend is gone who'd verify
we were ever in the Royal Danish Museum,
thirty winters past, staring at an antique oddity
in that furniture-clogged, third-floor room.
Just this image, lodged like a hardened pea
in memory's sieve. A globe set in a circular
table, but no map upon it. Multi-colored, spatter-

painted, Jackson Pollack-like — was it some
anomalous outbreak of Abstraction?
Or just a finicky Danish brush-wielder's notion
of a joke? Then—how suddenly this happened—
in the mirrored tabletop around the dome
blur became figure, the swirls straightened
into statues, flowers, a park in Copenhagen

and there was the sense of it, and the artifice.
And, by God, we got the picture. Today's mechanic
will regrind our Volvo's rotors while against the dryer's
wall my sneakers knock and bounce. Thus the years
recycle themselves: a quick shift in attention's orbit
and there I am, looking again. Only, say the colors switched
places in my mind. Now the globe's the polished

thing, with the tabletop's crazed designs reassembling
to images within the curves. It's just a ball. Go ahead, juggle it.
Look for a park in Copenhagen, statues, flowers
straightened into swirls. Then try to imagine a finite
universe. Nothing comes without pushing something
else out of the way. From the halls a voice calls
Ja visst, ja. A scrim of ice covers the canals.

A Native of Damascus Regards "The World Girls"—Two American Travellers, 1965

Wanderers, innocent of shoes
hurled by the shrieking wife

and easily lost, they are amazed
by the architectures of our belief,

the posters of our ruler
in all his readiness, larger than life.

Longing? Not a stance we'd confess
to daughters such as these, though they're naive

enough not to know whom to tell.
Memory tangles. If it comes, relief

is slow. Tiles click across the game board,
the patio, draped in vines, each leaf

a shadow of news. Dust layers
fruit that swells almost visibly, as if

crying taste to our tongue. They see
the bride behind her veil, cloth stiff

as custom or carved marble screens—
her intonations hushed, half

guessed, her sorrow mingling the air.
How shy we are, offering them our grief,

our intricate alphabet, rose-flavored
water from the clear carafe.

Inventing the Torch

(after a photograph by Manuel Alvarez Bravo)

Plaster wings outlined in torchlight,
the angel rides a truck
with solid tires.
At this pace, slats,
walls and truckbed dance
a strange processional over cobbled
stone. The torch
throws a wild light on bass clef
wings and the nose
in shadow suggests an angle
of inattention
as if, for him, the street
has simply faded
into its own distance.

Voice, whisper,
tell me what he apprehends—
the pedestrian clatter around him,
the trolley's empty hum? In truth,
I have invented the torch,
his quasi-human form.

Oh, there was an image once,
barely enough to think of now:
something moved through darkened streets
and an angel carried it,
small flame of memory—insistent, light.

What I Did Not Invent

I did not invent the seaside air or
the sleeping bag that split as we strolled
back to the train ready to leave Livorno
and spilled feathers as we picked up our pace,
running, breathless, for the platform, feathers
pouring, foaming around us, the bag ballooning
like an overgrown caterpillar or you,
arms outstretched like the Christ of Rio,
dropping it all on the floor of the car,
and me, making the best of it, stitching
the seams in a crowd of opinionated
Italians as the train lurched on.

Nor did I invent the night
we spread the bag under the impossible
Mediterranean stars. Not that I remember much,
but I did not invent more than that,
more than a satellite tracing a line
through those thick heavens, which for then
was new and extraordinary.
Oh, we embroidered our embarrassments
in two languages, took tea in small cafes
and hurled dissident songs against ancient walls
all hours of the night, before browsing
through morning markets opening to the sun.

I'm more settled now and sex is better
though decades in the rust belt leave me
with a certain fondness.   I remember chocolate
on the air and things Etruscan, even when
they weren't, and how we'd dance in basement bistros
and stay on the floor just to avoid paying
the next tab. My dancing clothes were tight,
green or black. Long red scarf. Thin flat shoes.
I wore my hair long and I'd sit in my window,
gaze into the valley and brush it at sundown.
I suppose I thought I was Rapunzel
but I'd never danced like that before.

Back home my generation crested into
maturity, but I fought it off. I was nineteen

and believed you when you told me
you were a poet, some things easier said
and done in another tongue. I wonder
what you think of me now: the girl who
went on to Sweden, *un'Americana,*
who did a few things well. None of this
is made up. Last night's dream of my husband
reminds me of you, but it's him I'm dancing with,
waltzing, spinning, as we turn and turn, faster, clear the floor.

V
IN THE STREAM

At the Victoria and Albert Museum

When the Zen master's brush was full, he'd hear an inking song.
These liquid lines let us in on his mind's unthinking song.

On a black lacquered boxtop, languid geishas limned in gold
strum drowsily downstream to catch the fireflies' winking song.

If Chihuly hadn't taken pains to hang these blown glass globes
just right, his *Tower of Light* would surely make a clinking song.

Does Samuel "Madam, you smell" Johnson stalk about these halls?
Methinks the air carries a tune: some body's stinking song.

Tipoo Tiger sets wooden teeth at an English captain's throat.
Crank up the hand-organ's tail to hear its bloody drinking song.

"Plaid words knot my babble," the young sari'ed poet wrote,
staring down the Scottish Guard through her unblinking song.

Outside, London is traffic, crowds, a global mix of tongues
converting *Rule Britannia* into a shrinking song.

Fellow travelers, make the most of artifacts and time
before your form runs out, like Tourist Blackhawk's linking song.

Force Fields

(Emily Carr, Canadian artist & writer, 1878—1945)

> *Stand still. The forest knows*
> *where you are. You must let it find you.*
> David Wagoner

i. Sky

"The subject is movement"
                —and sky: a rising
            surge of repetitions,
brush strokes like auras, arcs
rushing up
            through the undergrowth,
                    across the gravel pit
past loggers' culls
            beyond the vertical
                    spars of trees.

Today, Vancouver's children
pay crayon rainbow homage.
            To be an Emily, all you need
are bright, vibrating lines,
your vision drawn, as hers was,
                    onto fields of air.

Then file out
            of doors and down
the sunny walk. Never mind
                    her vanishing
hills, ridge upon ridge,
green brown to green black
to green blue—
            or the reverse
                    avalanche of clouds
                            outdistancing
the upthrust trunks, the roots'
            rock-splitting grip.

ii. Monkey Puzzle Tree
(Stanley Park, Vancouver, B.C.)

Serrated, drooping, with stiff
overlapping leaves,
each branch makes a *ristra* of knife-
edged, succulent stars.
A cactus in the rain forest?
One of her cubistic dreams?
Its palette spells restriction:
a dark, puritanical green,
but the underwater sea
creature it conjures casts about
in wild contortion.
Fiendishly snaking branches.
Medusa's tortured hair.
Independent. Don't touch! No other
of its kind on the continent.
A loneliness *"beloved,"*
she might have said, *"of the sky."*

iii. Totem
(Tsatsisnukwomi Village, 1907)

> *I slept in tents, in roadmakers' toolsheds, and in Indian houses. I*
> *travelled in anything that floated on water or crawled over land.*
>
> Emily Carr

No more the timid student, too shy
to view a naked model, you have come
up the coast by boat, alone,
and are not afraid now to sleep alone
in the emptied longhouse. You step gingerly
past banana slugs, dodge dozens
of famished cats that swirl underfoot
as you tramp the rotting plank walk
out to the edge of the abandoned Indian village.

There, through clouds of mosquitoes
and stinging nettles higher than your head,
you slip, fall before *D'Sonoqua*, woman
of the woods, stare stunned into the wild
oo's of her eyes, the black cavity
of her mouth, its breath filling the air
between the outstretched arms,
the dangling eagle-headed wooden breasts.

Easy sacrifice—if burning skin is all it takes
to find her, this towering totem, partner
of Raven, figure to warn children against.
Witch Woman, hungry, unappeasable, you
must paint her before moss and rain reclaim
the carved column of her neck, and the eyes
that echo through you as if you hear your own fear
beating inside her body's hollow drum.

iv. Bole,

or is it burl? the knot
on the trunk, the intensified
whorled source of pattern
in the wood. Then the unraveling,
the out-reaching. The knot as navel,
wrist, magic spot these new ribbons
of growth extend from. The witch
in the wood is breathing, extruding
a bouquet of scrawny spruce bones,
a root system grasping for air
twenty feet above the ground.

v. Sea

So this is how forest becomes sea—
a voyage the mind takes, anticipating
boundless waves, new
islands of light, the brush
stirring in its wake, the fingers tagging
clumsily along.

vi. Weather

Emily, old girl, you have us
bouncing through a whirl-
pool you long ago defined.
With what relish you frame
these tumults of clouds, boiling
eddies of sky, thunder
we can almost see
crumpling the canvas surface.

vii. Flesh

                Tempting to ask
why you would have none
of it, not Georgia's flagrant petals
or Frida's florid hearts. Why
you favored greens, not reds.
Not flesh but the mind home-
bound Emily knew was *wider than*
the Sky.   In love with trunks, fern,
bark, and *"air, high and fathomless,"*
fierce maiden abrupt gypsy sister
impatient with what you hadn't done,
bored with the rest, how can we
know you except for these coils
spurts and cascades of writhing
growth, a raw sexual force
your forests understand.

viii. Indian Basket

Between its earth-red stripes
a silver grass wind blows
like currents around a globe
in arrows of eastward-moving light.

She wants to breathe inside
its brittle flexibility,
immerse her face in its darkness,
leave it out in the rain,

then inhale the sweet grass smell.
Recalling Sophie, her basket-
maker friend, Emily strokes
the knobs grass makes crossing

over grass, thinks she might
dissolve at the edges
the way its curved sides
alter the space around it.

ix. Potlatch
(Victoria, B.C.)

          Teatime and the Bengal tiger
in the Kipling Room at the Empress Hotel
still sends its stuffed snarl through sun-
slatted afternoons, potted palms and lace.
Down the street, past the place of your birth,
herons fly from the park where you painted,
pass above your *House of All Sorts*
in their daily departure for the shore.
          Today, D'Sonoqua
stands display at the Royal Museum.
Klee Wyck the Haida name you, Laughing One.
But by the time you finish your *Potlatch Welcome,*
the Crown will already have banned
the dancers, locked up elders, grandmothers—
the gift of feasting forbidden, the art
of gifting abandoned—and all the weave
unraveled until Sophie's twenty babies
arrive half-starved and so silent the grave-
stone carver, not unkindly, calls her
his best customer, helps keep her tab
alive so she might place another marker
in the village's overgrown burying ground.

x. House
(1913-1933)

Scrub, rearrange, reorder and resign
yourself to *"reduced circumstance."*
The king's radio message New Year's Eve
still makes you cry. Crabby tenants.
Fix the plumbing, and the heat. In the center
of the ceiling paint eagles, still there,
Tlingit design. At last, pack your van. Collect
your menagerie. How many dogs? Add
boxes, sketchpads, your monkey and the rat.
Tighten canvas sides. Put the whole house-
hold on wheels. Now, leave. You're off.
You're old enough to bathe naked in the stream.

xi. Horizon

                              Rivers of air
fill your later canvases. Above the Strait
of Juan de Fuca, headlands you climbed
to sketch from, your skies unleash
their reverberating lines. What did you see
but magnetism, subatomic timbres,
currents you struggled to make visible
until the ethereal became too bright to bear
and you re-entered shadow and wood. Green
drape of cedar. A trunk's undulating stalk.
Regardless of horizon, all is swirling, fierce,
boring *"not down into darkness*
but through, into light."
                              Here—
these striated trees frame a birth canal
into the deeply scarred, deeply scarved dark,
your hand drawing the shawl of the forest,
coaxing her to lift her hem and let us in.

Parting the Waters

(after a series of paintings by Bob Barnes)

The yellow lines insist: *boat! boat!*
No dock or pier to anchor to—
but when I look into the tilting forms
        it seems I am floating
above a cove where tides suck and swell
     and there's this surge I'm riding
        whether I know it or not.

So when the guide says it's a beach scene
where three friends unearth poor Shelley's bones
and I find myself slipping on wobbly legs,
        it comes as no surprise.
I've boarded a boat that doesn't exist
     whose citrus backlight and huddled
        shades suggest cold

horizons and smoke from burning
cockleshell crafts the artist's ancestors used
in burials at sea. Last summer's sailboat
        returned unmanned, its lines
clanging, its captain's poems
     washed away. Small wonder
        I'm half-falling or flying,

snagged in the moment the foot stubs
a stair that wasn't supposed to be there—
books, bags suddenly airborne, the walls watery
        and trellises swaying
like spaghetti before it lands in your lap.
     And who's peering out from
        the next frame but Death,

with his raggedy stink, as if that x-rayed
zoot suit could make him the buck-toothed fall guy—
a skull-and-bones stand-in for...what? It's art nabs him.
        Let's applaud the move:
how he's flushed, out in the open, reaching for
     the box of exploding chocolates
        from the man with the artificial hand.

But the head's a wax disaster and the way

the floor rolls and the room tilts I know it's only
the sea again creeping in with its same old song.
                    Is this why my pulse
catches in my throat, throbs at my fingertips?
          But say the canvas *is*
                    a skin. Rub it, stroke it,

and a scent there, a perfume, a texture
or a tune...something rises. The artist names her
Snow White, tender Aphrodite, has her centered
                    in the foreground,
raising her arm to give the blessing of the sea.
          And I want to say yes
                    to all her apparitions,

to hear her humming not the ocean's cold refrain
but *summer sunlight supple grain* —
as if that language
                    of fruit and flesh
could help me breathe slowly,
          reel backward, retrieve
                    my fine drowned friend.

Listen. That ringing in the ears?
Drifting for days on the waves, it was all
the wanderer knew before he washed up on that shore
                    where poets routinely
sacrifice themselves, to be pulled
          at last from the deep
                    by the nets they've been unwinding.

And Now, This Small Poem

For three dollars anyone could have a vision.
Larry Levis   ("In 1967")

What floats forward floats back through the poem,
the one whose backwash stirs the shush/slur
of memory's waves. No, memory *waves*:
active weaver, rearranging lines, inverting sentences—

> *Arachne, taking liberties, was she weaver*
> *or just the consummate reader, pulling the sacred threads*
> *onto her own loom?*

Which brings us to the glow
of an orange, the slow motion opening of its skin,
how it drew the light to it, then sent it back out again
toward the overarching trees.

And how each drop of juice seemed like a point of fire
and *holy*—a word I borrow gingerly
from this poet of elegies and acid trips who helps me

follow my friend again, my LSD Girl Guide,
into a forest that was still the same yet suddenly
          not quite and more than the forest I knew.

          I was wearing my paisley skirt. I was blessing
each ritual slice she made in the orange.
I was listening to the spaces between the filaments

of a spider's web and feeling oh, such fellowship
with the spider and the sun illuminating
the singularities of the leaves. But if a few mandalas

stirred themselves to a slow dance on the surfaces of rocks
or trees, it was more Rabbit Hole than Revelation.
And where was Siva? Where, his crown of flames?

VI

FIRE DANCE

Emily's Bee

Stars are the apexes of what triangles?
Henry David Thoreau

Clover's too small for him
      but the beebalm's ample
petals present
      throat after throat of sweetness.
He's a rare centurion of bees,
        larger by a factor of ten
      than his fellows drifting by
and I like to think her lines
      bob with him—this languid yo-yo with his
        methodical drowse, probing
like a hummingbird the size
         of a masculine thumb.
     Black patent puppet with wild
yellow fuzz, unconcerned
     with *Pedigrees of Honey*,
      he turns blossoms to stanzas
    as controlled
and spasmodic as her own—
     and I'd see him as a messenger
from beyond the circles
    that confine us, the frames
     our hearts beat in.
So let the bumblebee triangulate: let's reverse light
      and dark and make him
   a benighted bobbing star
plucked out of time and placed
    in the space between us.
   What better connection
than a fat bee, one day in summer,
    casting random constellations
across a flower bed—
     a velvet calculus
      I can almost touch.

Touchstone

(after Sergei Eisenstein's "Alexander Nevsky")

A stone cannot be
taught to perform,
is mute, stiff

as the frozen
tongue of an ox.
What erases its story?

The field beyond
redemption, icy
silence, icy weeds—

perfect backdrop
for the czar
massing on the horizon,

the swarm
of followers praising
Him, the Redefiner.

Across the icebound lake
His troops rise
ready to cut

tongues, silence
the tellers—
a forest of helmets

and scissored
moons darkening
the illogical earth

and you there, empty-
handed, watching them
coming toward you

with nothing
but this bit of luck
in your pocket

this touchstone
you plucked at night
from the fire.

Marc Chagall's "Green Violinist"

His dreamy eyes stare not quite at us
but at some space behind our heads so we look away
from the whorled beard, the green face,

and gaze up into a series of segmented arcs
balanced point to point on the gables
of a long-ago *shtetl* — a geometry

of clouds and a man flying through them.
Perhaps this small suited soul with outstretched arms
is what the violinist sees, a homunculus

in air placed above the purple cap, heading out
beyond the frame. The violinist fills the frame,
but he is grounded in the village, small stuff

at his feet: a ladder propped against
a leafless tree, beige dogs barking up at him,
donkey braying. Does he hear echoes

from the chapel with its frescoes of the doomed
marching naked into the jaws of Hell?
Would he drown out *Frere Jacques* —

which mocks Jewish Jacob, not John —
with lullabies that let the boy dream on,
away from morning mass? His green

hand draws the bow. His white hand
grips the neck of the instrument
whose klezmered frenzy rises

through the scrolls and staves, the intersecting
planes of the player's purple coat. The song
ascends the pitched roofs, opens

the cabin windows. The cabin windows
open his song. Under a roiling moon
the beasts have escaped from their stalls,

while over the sleeping houses
a song in the guise of a man —
a man in the guise of a song — goes flying.

Against a Whiter Snow

(for Judy)

> *How neatening is loss, since it only takes away!*
> Mary Oliver

And what stubborn mess you add now, refusing to subtract,
here on the far edge of the illness you described last month

over Korean soup and mushrooms: the recurrence
you must gaze into, the abyss you will not let gaze back.

What better means of resistance than this melange of mortgage,
cat door, chimes for the new deck, stacks of logs for the stove.

In with the century! In with the new! You'll be a blizzard, a blur,
a moving mass of books, poems, sheet music, your husband's

crossword puzzle archive. It's almost enough to make me believe
in the serendipitous now, how the time arrived and the house

with it, the fire your downstairs landlady
might as well have set on purpose sending you scanning ads

until you found it — a nature preserve at its doorstep,
a hot tub in the garden and oh, at last, a window

over the kitchen sink. "The mail cheek-by-jowls a curious lot,"
you once wrote, in a jumble of language I loved.

Today's mail sets your New Year's news beside a homemade card,
a friend's snapshot, her white goat against a whiter snow.

I can barely make out the horns and beard, the wise animal eyes,
but I can see your scarred body sinking into fragrant steam,

your bare feet crossing scrubbed wood floors, rooms filling
with light and how mornings you will take coffee on your deck,

drain the ink from your pen and try your lines aloud to the tender
air, while high in the canopy birds will arrive on schedule

and nights an owl will call, helping you claim the dark.

For Dudley Randall-
(1914-2000)

During the after-funeral luncheon
when the conversation turned to healing,
I told how the doctor from Shanghai cured
my frozen shoulder, and how, on my sixth
or seventh visit, he described the burning
of his father's books—the father himself jailed,
the family persecuted by the Red Guard.

As the needles entered my skin, I didn't tell
about a different red, the red I followed
years before when red meant rage
against the machine, meant set suppressed
stories free. Red had me then, freezing
on street corners, sending a collective
challenge into the teeth of 5 a.m.

shift changes, trying to catch the eye or ear
of even one worker hurrying home
from forge or stamping machine,
sometimes willing to stop, buy a paper,
more likely glad to flirt with any young female
as I stood, feet numb, pulling out nickels
or dimes, brave red star on my coat—

while deeper in my city a man I never knew
was waging a new revolution with new words,
new names: Haki, Nikki, Sonia, Etheridge:
publishing from his storefront on Livernois
hundreds of volumes, broadsides, chapbooks,
distributing thousands of pages to make the world
Think Black! Jump Bad, fanning thousands of flames.

Once the needles were in, Dr. Wang touched them
with fire. Holding tiny cotton torches
delicately, with tongs, he conducted
his "needle dance" from point to metal point
until, I swear, my arm began to rise,
reaching for the middle of the air in a manner
as unpremeditated as Shelley's lark

or Ezekiel's wheel, or the sisters
and brothers at the service, their spontaneous

tributes recalling the poet as mentor,
fighter, seer, friend. Malaika rising
from her pew in *a capella* homage.
Ibn pouring libations on his grave.
What is the difference between will and intent?

Dudley, the dogma I pinned to my chest
dissolves in songs and stories
and I think of the phoenix you summoned,
how the faith you held in every voice lifts now
through these dozens of different incantations,
flashes of hope, like the bird's spangled feathers
drifting down across this ash-ridden town.

Duende

(after viewing the film "Flamenco")

...her dance begins to flicker in the dark room.
Rainer Maria Rilke

Call it passion or possession—
you'll find it in the thrust
of this ordinary man's scarred
jaw, the sharp golden spades
of his eight upper teeth, the camera
so close in you can almost see him tongue
the air. Don't be embarrassed.
Avoid the nervous snicker or smirk.
Listen to the voice—like a muzzein's
greeting the sun. Notice the mouth
distorted by its cry. Give in
and his song will exile you
to your own foreign lands
the way the Gypsies, Muslims,
Jews wandered then returned
bearing with them this mix
of diaspora and *duende*—-
music of soul in her extremis.
Here you are, face to face
with a man who could have pumped
your gas, cut your hedges, and he's
filling your space with an intimate
intensity. What to do but succumb
to his strung-out, wrung-out ur-song,
to the ravishing chords and the dizzying
dancer beside him spinning
on clacking feet. Look at them now,
urged on by family and friends.
A frenzy of hands sustains them,
a chorus of palms maintaining the beat
as her heels and his voice assert
their bodies' insistent fire.

Fire Dance

(after an installation of glasswork by Dale Chihuly)

Luminous, his seductive cherubs alight,
grinning, everywhere, squeezed into crevices,
riding chandeliers, polymorphic surprises
like eggs at an Easter hunt hidden in plain sight.

Some seem ready to burst into light or steam.
Heat must have done this, forged this illusion
of glass turned flesh as plump and golden
as it is innocent and full. As a boy he'd dream

into watery green, wandering the sand
on his Oregon shore, or drape across
dunes and let air fill him like water. Now his glass
waves like anemones, opened, pulsing, fanned.

Then, too, there had been the noontime lattices
of his grandmother's pergola to crane beneath
and find among shadows of grape or leaf
pendulous plays of light. Say that tremulousness

would remind him of lips,
of the girl he wanted to be his girl;
how he would watch her for what she could reveal
with her sudden impudent tongue;

or imagine him, breath stilled by bats
or moths, as if swallowing their flight. Ample
time then for a boy to indulge in simple
desires, to collect and sketch the best

in beachcombed detritus, sea urchin and shell,
abalone, balleen, or the finest toys—
Japanese fishermen's hand-blown buoys
carried on Pacific waves. These would tell

of the floating world, its lost women, red, red
lips and nights of song, songs the glass sings on the shelf,
seagreen songs of koto and flute and strands of kelp
tangled in long black hair. Faces powdered,

pale voices ringing in the glass, poor disembodied

ones, say he'd dream a fire into them, flesh
he'd twirl, mold, melt against, or press
to his mouth in waking sweat as waves subside.

Flesh of the sea gives a different texture
but he found these, too—sea slug and cucumber...
                            Relentless treasure—
how he has let it all body forth and figure

into the cherub he had always been—
a rampant imp, architect of light and desire
who from the sea came to admire
heat as origin: the molten matter at the end

of the gather spinning the breath
of the blower into the breath of the flame.

Amaryllis

A deep cold has lifted;
piles of snow recede.
Aging blooms on the first stalk

droop and turn sticky, then papery,
dry. Yet still the plant dances
as if around its own flame.

When my friend sent me this,
wrapped in florist's foil,
its name was not a flower
but a girl, some lost legend —

Opp, Amaryllis! Vakna min lilla —
scraps of tune frail as wilting
tulip blossoms, stained taffeta —
there, there, old girl.

But here's a gift to reclaim
the dark solstice, a present
that inclines us
toward one another's light.

A bulb's curve emerges
above the dirt. The wand
doubles, erupting into bloom.

Rise, Amaryllis! Wake up, my darling—
We startle at it, hushed
by this chorus of tissue and thrust—

four blossoms on one
stem, veined clarions,
wide-mouthed proclamations.

Notes

"Burmese Girls Sold into Prostitution in Thailand":
All quotes and information are taken from the P.O.V. documentary film "Sacrifice," produced by Ellen Bruno and aired on PBS, July 1998.

"...*the days when Birds come back...*" is written in memory of Denise Spence, 1944-1997.

"Teaching with Dickinson One Morning in Spring" is written in memory of Larry Pike, 1932-1995.

"Mediterranean Crossing":
Flee to the indifferent lifesavering shippen is taken from a Greek ferry's life boat instructions entitled "Help Savering Apparata." The entire instructions read: "In emergings behold many whistles. Flee to the indifferent lifesavering shippen, then associate the stringing apparata about the bosoms and meet behind."

"Force Fields":
All quotations and information are taken from Doris Shadbolt's *The Life of Emily Carr* as well as from *Klee Wyck*, *Growing Pains* and other writings by Emily Carr.

"Parting the Waters" is dedicated to the memory of Stephen Tudor, 1933-1994.

"Marc Chagall's "Green Violinist'":
According to an NPR report, *Frere Jacques* was originally an anti-Semitic song. Gustav Mahler, who had been forced to convert from Judaism to Catholicism in order to conduct the Vienna Philharmonic, included a mournful reworking of the tune in his first symphony's third movement.

"For Dudley Randall":
A pioneer in independent African-American publishing, Dudley Randall (1914-2000) founded Broadside Press in 1965, thus helping to open American publishing to black and other minority writers. Dudley Randall served as Poet Laureate of the City of Detroit from 1980 until his death.

"Fire Dance":
"Fire dance" is a term used to describe "the craftsman's movement of the molten glass in and out of the flame while shaping the bead." from *Lampwork Beads and Jewelry Brochure*.

Terry Blackhawk is executive director and founder of InsideOut
Literary Arts Project, a writers-in-schools program serving students in
Detroit's public schools. She is also the author of *Body & Field* and the
chapbook *Trio: Voices From the Myths*. A former Detroit high school
teacher, she holds a BA from Antioch College and a PhD from Oak-
land University. Her honors include the Foley Poetry Award from
America, a National Endowment for the Humanities Teacher-Scholar
Award, the Michigan Governors' Award in Arts Education, and a
Michigan Council for Arts & Cultural Affairs Artist-in-Residence grant.
She lives in Detroit with her husband, Evan. A webpage for Terry
Blackhawk can be found at www.poets.org under "Find a Poet."